Think in Decades

Hearing God While Drumming Mute

Morgan Gascho

First printing 2021.

Table of Contents

Dedication

I dedicate this book to my basketball girls, who became the audience and inspiration I needed to complete this book.

Lulu, thank you for leaving a legacy of love and joy through the generations of your family. You are incredibly life giving!
Dana, you were born for greatness! You will always be part of this family.
Anni, you're hilarious! For the record, you have great hair! Now it's in ink!
Adah, the Father said He was pleased in His Son before He started His public ministry; and the Father was proud of you before you did anything amazing. I am proud of you and continue to be amazed by your skill and character. Keep your head up, champ.
Autumn, your boldness on the court inspires us, and your organization off the court pushes me to be better. Thank-you for bringing your whole self.
Ayla, you are a storyteller and a creative at heart. May you continue to create many beautiful things in your life and may you leave a legacy far greater than you ever dared to believe.
Bauer, you will always be enough. You already are. Bauer power!
Ava, seeing you walk in confidence and in your true identity has been one of my life's greatest joys! You are amazing, and you are loved more than you know!

Charlie, you are meek, honest, and trustworthy. You are the real deal and are full of character. I would have you on my team any day. Thank you for being a team player and an amazing leader.

Cora, You have a beautiful vigor for life that is seen most when you are truly yourself. May the Lord strengthen you to walk in wild and crazy boldness all your days!

Emma, thank you for always being willing to pray for and love your teammates. Your heart for Jesus and your teammates blesses my heart.

Lydia, you were "born to win"! We really could make a t-shirt! May that fiery confidence remain within you forever.

Melody, God has anointed you with joy beyond your companions, because you have loved righteousness and have hated lawlessness. (Hebrews 1:9) You are fun to be around, and we enjoy you!

Noelle, I'm pyped! Your presence and leadership has been a blessing. Your character and wisdom is admirable. We love you with all our hearts!

Peyton, may your passion for greatness never dim and may you continue to grow in the wisdom you already carry so well. You are a great leader, and you lead with honor.

Acknowledgments

I acknowledge and thank God for always giving, always being generous, and for always being a good Father. Thank You for giving me a story and for giving me the words to share it. You are amazing, and I'm glad I will be with You forever.

To my mom and dad, thank you for championing me to write and for helping me edit my first published book! To my basketball girls, thank you for being the motivation I needed to complete this book. Thank you, Laura, for watering the seed that had been planted in my mind but not yet sown. Thank you, Kirste, for championing me as a writer and for understanding and encouraging the heart behind the writing. Thank you, Kelli, for believing in me and for speaking out that I am a good storyteller. Thank you, Lindsey, for hearing from the Lord and delivering the *Think in Decades* word. I love you all and receive your love and encouragement!

Preface

Storytelling Like God

The reason I am writing this book is multifaceted. Firstly, testimonies are a Biblical tool to help us overcome the enemy. (Revelation 12:11) I am mirroring my Creator when I become a storyteller, and I am joining in what Heaven is already doing by valuing people's stories. We'll delve more into the details of the "why" behind the "what", but if you're like me and want to get to the point, skip to the introduction!

Heaven Values My Stories

One main reason for writing this book is because Heaven values my stories. This statement doesn't come from haughty or self-righteous thinking; rather it comes from a confidence that I am aligned with Jesus when I agree with Him about the things He says are true. I want to be as free as possible, and I know the Truth sets us free; thus my agreement with Him sets me up to walk in freedom.

I used to work in a house of prayer, where the days were often spent in the windowless prayer room, walking and praying, listening to God, reading Scripture, leading prayer and worship sets, or interceding for people who walked in through the heavy, glass doors. Praying with and for people was oftentimes encouraging, but more frequently, the Lord and His invited Heavenly host and myself were the only ones in the room.

On one specific day, when no others were in the room, I walked back and forth from the eastern entrance to the western wall of the prayer room, behind the last row of maroon chairs facing forward toward the stage. I prayed silently to the Lord as I walked, and I remember talking to God about how I was hesitant to share my testimony. The Lord replied quickly, corrected my thinking, and reminded me my story was not my own but was His. He was not controlling, nor was He domineering, but in a gentle tone, He reminded me I'd made Him Lord over my life and had given Him control. I repented (changed my thinking), and agreed with Him that my story was His to share. I confessed that if it brought glory to Him or brought joy to His heart, it was my honor and joy to share it. That's one reason behind the writing of this book. It's a simple act of obedience to share my testimony and story, because I believe it will bring a smile to God's face.

For the Sake of Victory

The second reason I am writing this book is for the sake of victory. I've seen in Scripture how the Lord has given us two accessible tools to overcome the accuser of the brethren. These two tools include the blood of the lamb and the word of our testimony.

> **Then I heard a loud voice in heaven say:**
> **The salvation and the power and the kingdom of our God and the authority of His Messiah have now come, because the accuser of our brothers has been thrown out:**
> **The one who accuses them before our God day and night.**
> **They conquered him by the blood of the lamb and by the word of their testimony, for they did not love their lives in the face of death.**
> **Therefore rejoice, you heavens, and you who dwell in them! Woe to the earth and the sea, for the Devil has come down to you with great fury, because he knows he has a short time. (Revelation 12:10-12)**

If the blood of the Lamb plus the word of our testimony is what conquers the enemy, I don't take these ingredients lightly.

This is another reason why I cannot and do not neglect sharing testimonies. It's not only for the hearers' exhortation and encouragement, but is also for the sake of my own heart remembering who I am and what the Lord has done in and through me. It aligns me with my identity. It aligns me with Jesus.

Mirroring My Creator

Thirdly, in becoming a storyteller, I am mirroring my Creator, Jesus. He was a great Storyteller, and showcases this through many of the parables in the Gospels. Families of men, women, and children came to Jesus to hear His teachings, but they were not all scholarly and learned like the Pharisees. His stories were relevant to everyone, were easy to listen to, and were easily shareable. This is part of what makes Jesus' teachings relatable. They were simple for those who had an open heart and open ears. They were stories of Truth, made to set people free, in a format everyone could digest. It was the simple Gospel.

I want to become a storyteller in the same sense, being able to relate to many different people and being all things to all people. I want to communicate to young and old and to those who grew up in the church and to those who didn't. These stories aren't for the sake of arguing theology or proving God did something at some point in my life. They're for the sake of sharing my heart and my experiences. They're for the sake of carrying on a legacy and sharing that God can and will do greater things through the next generation and those who come after me. These are stories to encourage spiritual growth and faith, and they're shared to be publicly celebrated. With that, take these testimonies and share them with someone who might need to hear them to be encouraged.

I once heard our University campus pastor say any testimony about God that he hears becomes his own, because he can then use those stories to encourage someone at a later time. The same is true of these testimonies. Feel free to share these stories after you hear them and feel free to use them to speak encouragement to another. They are not my own. They are the Lord's testimonies. I give away what He freely gave me.

Leaving a Legacy

The last reason I am writing this book is to leave a legacy for my girls. Since I was young, I wanted to read writings by friends and family members. I have always been intrigued by other people's experiences and thoughts and I want to know other people's stories. I want to hear how they grew up, what their days are like, and what they think of their everyday world. What might seem mundane or normal to them are things I am intrigued by. Milking cows, waking up in the morning to ride the bus to school, playing football at the local stadium, and doing chores on the farm are everyday occurrences that I want to know about. I am eager to gain knowledge from past and present generations.

Kids today are no different. Everyone hungers to know. We were made in the image of God. We were made to gain knowledge and run with it. I want to write to fill dreamers' minds with thoughts of impossible adventures, that they might fulfill some and dream of more. I want to write to leave a legacy for present and future generations.

I pray the writings bless you, encourage you, and bring you hope. May you grow to receive love more fully. May you fulfill Jesus' words and do greater things than Jesus. (John 14:12) May the eyes of your heart be enlightened to the hope of His calling, the riches of His glorious inheritance in the saints, and the surpassing greatness of His power to those who believe. (Ephesians 1:18-19) May blessings upon blessings be upon you and your family. I bless your soul, spirit, and body in Jesus' name. Amen.

Introduction

"The Lord gave me a word for you. He said to think in decades."

My friend told me this, years ago, when I was frustrated about the lack of movement toward my life goals. I wanted to know when God would catapult me and connect me with my tribe of like-minded people who had the same vision, calling, and anointing. I was entirely caught up in the future, I was frustrated with the Lord's timing, and I wasn't enjoying the present moment, likely because it felt like an eternal waiting room. This is when I thought it was a good idea to pray for patience.

I've learned from this experience. Ever since I heard the following story of a woman who prayed for patience, I find it hilarious to do the same, because I don't know how the Lord, in all His grace and humor, will answer my prayer. There was a woman who prayed for patience who received her answer through the beautiful gift of eight children. In my mind, there's no way her patience did not grow, as she lived with more than eight beautiful souls who required daily needs from her. The Lord sure did answer her prayer. That is one reason why I am careful and intentional in what and how I pray.

Instead of demanding, I've learned to wait. I've learned to sit before the Lord, to wait on Him, (Lamentations 3:25-27) and to consider it a blessing to speak and to listen. I've learned that prayer is a two way street, and that the Lord really does want to partner with me when it comes to establishing His Kingdom on earth.

A few months ago, I was at a job I did not enjoy; and I prayed to God, reminding Him of the passion He's given me for missions, to go to unreached people groups, to be a part of making His name known on the earth, and to belong to a group of people who beckon His return. I reminded Him of His Word that says the disciples were sent out two by two. I reminded Him how I had ventured out by myself years before and how it had not turned out great. I told Him I'd learned my lesson, and that is when I asked Him to connect me with another person who has a similar heart and vision to go across the world and to do His will.
A few months later, I received an answer to prayer through the text of a friend. The text message asked if we (my roommate and I) were looking for a third roommate, and frankly, I wasn't; but for whatever reason (the grace of God), I told my friend I'd be willing to meet with this girl anyway.

It's funny telling this story in hindsight, as I now have a new best friend and a completely different plan than I did seven months ago. Long story short, the prospective roommate whom my friend texted about ended up moving in, and we discovered we both love sports, children, health, Jesus, missions, worshiping, writing, and a myriad of other interests that make a difference in choosing life long friends.

This last season of life has been a whirlwind of Jesus connecting us to one another and connecting us to ideas of Heaven. With that, the Lord has also resurrected dreams He birthed in me years ago.

Chapter 1: Fifth Grade Chapel

We were in chapel in my school's gym, and I was sitting in the back right corner near the volleyball pole, beneath the wide upper level windows. The guest speakers were young people, full of energy, hope and visible passion. I engaged with their intensity, because they brought with them a tangible presence of God.

Multiple expressions of worship filled this chapel service, and I especially engaged with the music and dance offered as an incense arising. I was drawn in by the unfamiliar look and deep beats of the djembe (a hand drum that has become one of my favorite instruments to play in worship sets), though I didn't know what it was at the time. I sat wide-eyed, watching the joyful dancers move across the stage beautifully, swaying and giving visual expression to the utterances of the Holy Spirit. Inspired in hearing testimonies from one of the young adults in the group, my heart leapt at the chance that some day I could be doing the very same thing, bringing hope and encouragement and igniting fires in the hearts of young people all over the world. Tangible courage filled my body as my heart was set ablaze for overseas missions that day.

Since then, I have kept these things hidden in my heart, and I have never been the same. At the end of chapel, the team handed out pamphlets, which for me became a prop of a cherished moment with the Lord. When at home, I carefully placed this pamphlet in my "special box", where sentimental moments of written letters, photos, and journal entries were stored. This pamphlet was a reminder of how God met me in that chapel service. It was a reminder He had spoken to me about my calling, to go overseas and to join in His cause of making disciples all over the earth. (Matthew 28:16-20) Every so often or when reminiscing in my special box, I would pull it out and would be reminded of what the Lord had burned on my heart. I wanted to go to the nations.

I'm not sure if I had verbal explanation for everything God did in my heart on that day, but that chapel was significant to me. I encountered God. He spoke to me about my purpose. I was in fifth grade, and I had a real encounter with God. I knew He was speaking to me, and I felt His passion burning in my heart very clearly. This is one reason I know the Lord speaks to kids and adults alike. He can move on our hearts when we are any age. There really is no such thing as a Junior Holy Spirit.

From then on, I had hope and passion. I knew there was a storyline written by God that I had yet to discover and experience. My prayer was to receive His love in a tangible way, to love Him and people well, and to be used by Him. I wanted to join in on the storyline He'd begun. I wanted to live out the story He was writing. I wanted Him to complete in me what He had started.

"I am sure of this, that He who started a good work in you will carry it on to completion until the day of Christ Jesus." (Philippians 1:6)

Chapter 2: 8th Grade Decisions

When I was in 8th grade I wanted to go to the movie theatres with my friends, and I approached my dad to ask him if it was plausible. I gave him all the specifics of our plan, because I knew he'd be more likely to say 'yes' if I gathered all of the detailed information and then asked him.

He informed me the movie was one he didn't think my friends and I would enjoy and he didn't think it was a good idea. I listened as he told me, but my desire to be with my friends trumped my perceived value of his advice. He gave me freedom to go to the movie and didn't shame me for making my own decision.

I went to the theatres, and my friends and I all found our way to the seats, happily embracing our newly found, independent teenage freedom. Within minutes we found ourselves oddly uncomfortable with the foul verbiage, crude jesters, and impure motives conveyed on screen. Looking over at one another in disgust, we agreed the money spent for the ticket was worth losing to gain back time we'd rather spend differently. We ditched the movie. Happy to leave with peace of mind and a clear conscience, I realized my dad was right. The movie wasn't worth it.

One thing I learned from this experience was how to make choices. I believe I learned more from making a choice and seeing the consequences than I would have if my dad would have told me no. In giving me freedom, he was honoring my ability to discern and to choose not even what was right or wrong, but what was best.

As a good father, the Lord also does this. He gives us the gift of responsibility for our actions. He doesn't always just say a black and white 'yes' or 'no'. He gives us choices wrapped in freedom.

I unexpectedly learned this while in university. I remember calling my mom in college, somewhat frazzled about making a decision and being frustrated I didn't hear a clear answer from the Lord regarding what to do. As she and my dad often do, she operated in wisdom and advised me that the Lord doesn't always tell us what to do and that He sometimes gives us choices, because He trusts us more than we trust ourselves.

This baffled me, but the truth resonated. I knew she was right. The Lord was intentionally growing and maturing my trust, not only in Him, but also in myself, in order that I could make decisions and own the consequences, whatever the outcome.

Chapter 3: Sophomore Year Perspectives

I believe this is why in my sophomore year of university the Lord gave me choices. I attended a class called Perspectives on the World Christian Movement, where different missionaries came weekly to share their personal testimonies of life on the mission field. Every Sunday, I came to class, eager to hear the stories and to know what God was doing in the nations; and many times I ended up on the phone with my mom, crying about how I wanted to take a gap year and go to the mission field. I knew it was my calling, but I didn't know the details of when, how, or why.

I felt intensely and deeply, and the Lord was stirring me, but I didn't have the words to help contextualize it. I was touched by God, but I didn't yet have language. I knew there was something beautiful about Africa and that my heart was stirred to go. This was the puzzle piece I had.

These phone calls to my mom and dad became routine, and my friends got sick of me talking about Africa and street children and people living in poverty. I even exhausted myself with an overload of information. My heart was on fire, and I grew in zeal, but I needed balance. Graciously the Lord provided that by helping me to grow in wisdom and discernment.

Taking Perspectives class my sophomore year at UNI stirred up my desire for missions, but because I didn't see quitting university as a viable option, I figured I could at least get some cultural experience overseas. This is what led me to study abroad in South Africa during my junior year.

Chapter 4: Unexpected and Teachable Moments

It's now helpful to know that when I make a decision, I go all in. Thus, I didn't sign up for just one semester; I signed up for the whole school year at Nelson Mandela Metropolitan University. My local school, the University of Northern Iowa, had just recently connected with Nelson Mandela Metropolitan University in South Africa, and this was the first year students were traveling there to study abroad. Typically students go for one semester, especially when it's a brand new program, but I was excited and felt more than ready to be in Africa. It had been my dream since fifth grade, and I felt like I was finally making progress in fulfilling the dreams of my youth.

I was full of zeal and excitement when I called my mom from the Chicago airport, telling her that I was going to South Africa and if I didn't come back she was welcome to come visit me. I was on cloud nine! The plane ride consisted of beautiful sunsets and sunrises seen from the 15-inch window separating sanity and sky, along with daydreaming in and out of changing sleep schedules. I'm not sure if it was the tiredness from jet lag or the irony of not knowing what to do, but when we arrived at the South African airport, gathered our things, and recognized no one was there to pick us up, the other international student with me started to panic. As is my typical reaction to most things, I found the situation hysterical and couldn't stop laughing. Here we were in a South African airport having no idea where the school was or where we needed to go, and we didn't have a working phone to communicate with anyone. I knew the Lord had provision for us, and that was my safeguard, thus panic mode seemed like a waste of time and energy. She, unfortunately, did not get as good a laugh out of the situation. To each their own.

A sighting of a telephone pole brought her solace, and we ended up calling someone. If I remember correctly, due to my slaphappy state, I couldn't hold it together long enough to stream out a coherent sentence, thus I think she called. To this day I don't know whom she called or how that helped, but eventually someone did come. After almost everyone from our flight had been picked up, a tall, well built man whistled in stride with his walk, with the gold watch on his wrist resting in his long-legged, black pants pocket. Seeing us, he asked if we were the international students heading to NMMU. We nodded, agreeing this may be our ride, and without an extra word, he turned and told us to follow him to the van. Hoping this was the correct transport and ride, we wheeled our luggage to the car. With no paperwork needed and time now being a concept outside of westernized clocks on the wall, my first experience in South Africa had begun. Little did I know, the year would continue with many more unexpected and teachable moments.

Chapter 5: The Rock Wall

One experience at the beginning of the year was incredibly memorable, but I would not categorize it as hilarious. The international students did not know each other from Adam when we first arrived, and the school was strategic in introducing all of us to one another. To do this, they rallied us all for an overnight retreat where we enjoyed activities like outdoor rock wall climbing, storytelling, and camping. The rock wall was a hit! We climbed outside, under the bright sun, as our new acquaintances sat on the dusty, brown clay-like dirt to watch our attempts to reach the top.

I watched one of the tallest European students climb first, and being lanky and agile, he quickly made his way to the top of the rock wall. His length benefited him as he ascended, skipping many of the holds that most short people would need. His time and speed was impressive and probably would have been a record, until I saw him three fourths or more of the way up, struggling for his grip. With one hand on the wall, he attempted to use momentum from his legs to reach for a different hold with his other hand; but he missed the grip, and the unexpected happened. The clip attached to the carabineer snapped in two, and in what seemed like slow motion and breath stopping tragedy all at the same time, he fell right in front of me onto the ground.

His girlfriend and the rock wall specialists ran to his side to aid him, and I, half in shock, calmly stayed seated and prayed under my breath that we would see a miracle. I thought he might have a concussion or a broken back, but nothing was determinable without medical care. I remember thinking this might be a moment why I was there, to pray for him and see a miracle and experience revival within our first few days!

I honestly don't remember much else of that retreat other than a few food discoveries, mostly from how Europeans eat cheese and jam on toast or how they eat granola hot, cold, or with both milk and yogurt simultaneously. I found these options fascinating, tried them myself, and became hooked on these snacks. They actually came in handy a lot that year, as I discovered a new survival skill I'd soon need to learn and incorporate into my daily routine in order to survive. It was called food prep.

Fortunately, the school had a few places where we could purchase food, and though it was delicious, it was expensive for a college student's budget; but that wasn't my only concern. I was nervous about the campus monkeys stealing my lunch. I had seen one too many innocent students get chased with lunch in hand, only to become a victim to monkey thieves. I must confess it's somewhat like a scene on "America's Funniest Home Videos" where you know the end result but laugh anyway. It never did get old watching someone's lunch fly into the air as they ran away from a troop of campus monkeys. It was good comic relief during study breaks, but I didn't want to be the one providing the entertainment.

One of my best friends didn't mind, though. I tried to warn her, but she was a stubborn French woman who had fallen in love with South Africa's beauty and nature. She was studying zoology, loved animals, and thought a picnic with the monkeys would be a good 'connecting with nature' moment. She sat down in the middle of their typical territorial area, and they slowly began coming up to her. She offered them small pieces, talking to them as they came up one by one. It was a great 'connecting with nature' moment, until one of them bit her, after which some French words came out, some of which I'm sure were no longer affirmations.

It's moments like these that make an international student easily stick out. Unexpected, hilarious, and teachable moments became a norm. Never once did I see a South African native sit with the monkeys. Point taken.

A few days after our retreat, the international students gathered at a rally. There I saw the tall, lanky, European student who fell from the rock wall. He seemed well and was walking around with his friends with a cast on one arm. The school publicly recognized him for being a trooper and rewarded him a well-deserved, free t-shirt.

Chapter 6: Ubuntu

There weren't many free hand outs in South Africa, and the t-shirt was a bonus gift for our classmate; but I got a free lesson in Ubuntu the day my classmate spoke up in a lecture hall, asking the teacher for a different test date due to a death in the family. She had a funeral to attend and the dates coincided with an upcoming class exam. The teacher responded to the girl by asking the class if they would all be willing to switch the date of the exam to help this girl. I wondered if it was out of genuine kindness or out of wanting to delay the exam, but all of the students complied and agreed that a later date would be appropriate.

Never before nor since have I seen the reaction that happened afterward. The teacher asked the students near the girl to comfort and console her, and a classmate to the right of her stood up in our 200+ lecture class and started to sing! She sang beautifully, passionately, and genuinely, giving my classmate the space and permission needed to express grief and mourn her loss. It was a public, communal expression of compassion and grief, giving room to breathe and to be a human, even in the middle of a university lecture class.

I sat stunned, interpreting this new experience in my Western cultured brain. The teacher called me out in front of the 200+ other students (a common occurrence, as she liked to use my obvious differences in nationality for teachable moments) to explain Ubuntu. Fortunately, I was paying attention in class and was able to engage whenever she called on me. This time, though, I had no answers for what was happening.

The teacher proceeded to tell me I was seeing and experiencing Ubuntu, which is the compassion and recognition of humanity. It was something they practiced in their culture, and though I didn't understand the word at that time, I understood the concept. I had seen humans regard one another as people and take a moment to support each other in time of need. I didn't know how much of a foretelling moment this was for me then, as I didn't know I would be clinging to Ubuntu in future days and months ahead on my own personal journey of recovery and healing.

Chapter 7: Distracted in Class

My classmates and I got to our seats before the bell rang, unlike other classes where we lingered until the last minute to get settled. This was an engaging, conversational group of students, all ready to learn, listen, and share perspectives. I typically loved this class, as I was naturally interested in the topics, which ranged from racism, religious differences, stereotypes, and judgments. The conversations were often unresolved at the end of the class; because we all engaged in deep thought, sharing perceptions from our own worldviews.

This particular day we sat, just like the other days, in a circle, facing inward toward one another; but this day I struggled to see people, hear comments, and focus on responses. It was neither my eyesight nor hearing, nor was it their volume or appearance that created the distraction. My mind was not present in that room. My thoughts were elsewhere.

I didn't realize my own headspace until one of my classmates turned to me, asked me my thoughts, and said she was curious to know my opinion. She thought it'd be interesting to have an American, a foreigner speak on the topic. Her valuing my thoughts and opinions honored me, but I didn't even know what she was talking about. I answered honestly, saying I didn't know what to say and was distracted at that moment, processing something that had happened within the last few days. In the natural flow of that class, more questions came from classmates and the teacher regarding what I was processing, what happened, and how I was doing.

Chapter 8: The Story

Knowing this may not be appropriate in other classes I'd taken, but fully embracing the moment, I explained that I'd been in the school for almost a year and that I was currently in my second semester of classes. Because of the length of time I'd been in the area, I was able to build relationships with people who lived near my housing location. The first semester I lived in a university dormitory, which was close to the beach and across the street from a convenience store. The store sometimes ran out of basic necessities like milk, coins, or cash, and they often needed runners to go to another nearby store to pick up these items. The store managers didn't want to run the errands themselves, as they'd lose business and abandon the cash register. They needed to attend to customers and stay in the shop. This issue was resolved through employing runners, who were often street kids, run the errands for them; and in return, the street children would receive small amounts of money. This was acceptable and common in the culture, as the street kids were given a sense of belonging and worth in the community through fulfilling these roles.

Because the store was right across the street from where we lived, it was convenient for us to run down to grab bread, milk, or a quick snack. We went there often, and would see the street kids who doubled as runners for the store. My Swedish roommate and I didn't speak any of the South African languages they spoke, and their English was better than our attempts at Xhosa or Zulu, thus we usually communicated with the boys in English. They were boys between the ages of around 11 and 18. They didn't know their exact age, and if they did, we didn't understand them when they told us. Either way, age didn't matter and we started to build a relationship with them.

We would go to the beach and they would show off, doing soccer tricks, back flips and all kinds of acrobatic moves that make most mothers nervous. They loved to play soccer, and in our attempts to play, they had fun and we sweated through a good workout. It was a win-win. We loved to walk about a mile down the road, to the boardwalk with them, where we'd play arcade games, eat samosas, and sometimes catch a movie at the local cinema. At one point they came over to our apartment and played music with us on my newly purchased djembe. Hanging out with the boys captures some of the most enjoyable times we had that first semester. I felt the spirit of adoption fill my heart, and I knew this was an overflow of the love of God pouring out.

There was a young South African Afrikaans man, whom we'll call Travis, who also knew the Lord, and he'd been building relationships with the boys, as well. He checked on them on a regular basis, and tried to get them into programs and educational systems in order that they could learn and go to school. He didn't want to see them end up in the townships or turn to addictions to cope with the trauma they'd experienced.

The boys were the ones who introduced us to Travis, and they went to church with him regularly. One Sunday, they invited us to come along, and we enjoyed one of the most freeing and fun rides I had ever experienced. We met the boys on the ocean front sidewalk and hopped into the back of Travis' yellow bakkie (truck) with them, hair flying in the wind all the way to the church building. It sounds country, but it actually took place in one of the biggest cities I've ever lived in, Port Elizabeth, home to one million people.

These experiences and times with the boys were memorable, and I have more good memories than bad ones; but the truth is there was a lot of trust given and a lot of trust broken. Unfortunately, the boys didn't have people protecting and taking care of them, like some kids do. We don't know where their mothers and fathers were, and we don't know if they had mothers and fathers living. If the boys had families, they may have lived in a township far away. Because of this, the boys felt the need to fend for themselves. They were their own family, trusting in one another for protection and provision. They had a tight bond, and I almost always saw them together. There were four boys we spent the most time with, named Vuyo and Siya, Given, and JJ. There were others they introduced us to, but those four were some of the core. Siya and JJ were brothers, Siya being the elder of the two. He was likely around age 14 and JJ around 11 years old.

One day when it was raining, light enough to walk outside but heavy and cold enough to need a jacket, we came across the boys as we walked on the sidewalk. They told us JJ had become sick, had gone to the doctor and had received a diagnosis for cancer; however, we do not know the accuracy of that claim. It was more likely that JJ fell ill due to illegal attempts to suppress his appetite.

We had compassion and brought him home in order that he could have a warm shower, some food, and some rest on the couch. He stayed for a night or two and seemed much better after he got cleaned up and ate something. It was a simple fix, and we were glad he was doing better. Sunday morning came around, all my roommates were out of the house, and I prepped to go to church. We had a special service that week, holding the gathering at the Boardwalk on a Sunday morning instead of our usual evening service at the university campus. This made it easier for me, as the Boardwalk was within walking distance. It'd be a perfect opportunity for JJ to join, since we could walk there together.

When I walked into the living room, JJ was busy watching sports on the TV. I asked if he wanted to come to church, but he was more into the game on the television. When I double-checked to make sure, he said he wanted to stay. I left the house, went to the campus church ministry, just a short walk away, and surprisingly enough, saw Vuyo there!

I didn't know he would be there, and I was excited to see him! With one lens piece missing from his black eye glasses, he spotted me easily and walked toward my spot at a seat in the front row. My smile brimmed wide, with pride of my new younger brother joining us for a public worship service that morning at the Boardwalk. We stood side by side, worshiping at the top of our lungs, singing in multiple languages, most of which I didn't know or understand. For the first time, I saw Vuyo worship with people who spoke his culture and dialect, and my heart felt thankful to God that he was able to experience worshipping God with other believers and singing in his own language. He lit up in a way I hadn't seen before, and I wondered if he was experiencing fellowship with the Lord.

After church, Vuyo and I tagged along with some of the international students who headed back to their dorm. As they ventured upstairs, Vuyo and I stayed outside, sitting on a wooden, horizontal fence beam underneath the warm sun. We chatted about important things like family, purpose, and God, and I was blown away at the level of the most in-depth conversation we'd ever had. There was intensity, honor, and authenticity in the conversation. Other than the language barrier, we were really beginning to understand each other. We were creating a bond. I wondered what God was up to, and I knew the Lord was working in all of our hearts. Thankful for the day, I realized the time by the color of the sky and the cooling of the night, and qualified it as late enough to start walking home.

Being about a mile or more away from the apartment, Vuyo offered to walk with me. Knowing the area and it's tendencies for thievery and violence, I gladly accepted. We made it back home safely, and when we walked into my apartment, many of the doors were open and the lights were on. No one was home, including JJ, and I figured he'd become bored and had left, wanting to be with his friends.

Vuyo asked if I was scared, and shaking my head, I asked, "No, why would I be scared?"

I didn't think about this again until later, but in hindsight that was an interesting question. I don't know if it was implied that I should be scared, if he was trying to be protective, or if he was asking if I was scared of him. Whether it was innocence, naivety or the grace of God, fear was not an issue for me.

I invited him into the house to continue our conversation in the living room, and during our chat I remembered something I wanted to show him on my camera. I walked out of the living room, turned right into the hallway and made a quick left, passing the colorful decorations I'd sticky taped to my bedroom door. Looking in the drawer where I kept the camera, I became perplexed, wondering where else it would be. I didn't find the camera, but I did see the drawer open. I closed it and looked around toward my closet to see the doors open, as well. This was not a typical thing, as I usually kept my belongings tidy with the closet and dresser drawers closed. I dismissed it and didn't think much of it, and went out into the living room to tell Vuyo that JJ must have borrowed the camera and that I could get it from him later.

We talked late into the night, and I was in awe of how much Vuyo opened up about his life. He began sharing things with me that, to this day, is still somewhat unbelievable. I shared a conversation in my apartment living room with a young boy, known as a street kid, who was teaching me, through his own story, about trafficking.

Chapter 9: Back in Class

I experienced Ubuntu for myself when my classmates and teacher showered me with verbal affirmations and support. They listened to my story, affirmed my feelings, and were vulnerable in sharing their own stories of feeling scared and violated. They told me it was normal to feel insecure and scared after having someone invade your home and steal from you. They reminded me a lot had happened and that I had been kind, but cannot trust everyone in the city, especially those who are used to fending for themselves as a lifestyle. They offered support and space to heal and breathe in that time, and I experienced my own lesson on Ubuntu.

It was incredibly healing to have that time of debrief with them, and it was completely unplanned, which helped all the more to know it was authentic and from genuine hearts. It was strange to feel like the entire school knew about it, because when class ended, I walked down the hall, still in shock from everything that had taken place. Left and right, students came up to me, some whom I had never met, giving affirmations and consolations about the unfortunate situation that had occurred. My guess is my roommate, who was in a classroom just down the hall, had a similar experience in sharing the story and receiving classmates' support.

This common space of having permission to be human and having time and space to process was both profound and healing. I'm thankful I was able to talk about the encounter in that class, because it was the most honest response I could give at that moment. I was given permission to be in process and to be fully human, complete with emotions and a soul.

Chapter 10: Wanting Familiarity

I'm not sure if it was days or weeks after the incident that I ran into the boys as we were out walking somewhere on the street. They greeted me with kindness and repeatedly apologized for JJ's bad behavior and how it impacted us. They said they didn't know where he was or where the stolen items ended up, and I wondered if this was true.

The rest of the year is somewhat of a blur, and I don't remember much of it. I know I was excited to come back to the states and experience familiarity, and the end of the year felt like it couldn't come fast enough. Though the ocean was beautiful, the scenery was breathtaking, and this was all within a few minutes walk from my living accommodations, my heart couldn't engage in the scenic beauty. I was done. I felt defeated, and I was ready to come home without a win.

Chapter 11: Re-Entry

I don't know if I've ever appreciated the beauty of Iowa as much as I have until that plane ride back into Cedar Rapids. It smelled familiar, felt familiar, sounded familiar, and everything was in a context I understood. I understood English. I understood driving on the right side of the road. I understood social cues of eye contact, appropriate spacing between customers in the grocery aisle, and friendly waves at four way traffic stops. I understood the Iowan way, yet coming home, I was different than when I had left.

I know people go through culture shock even upon returning to their original home, and this was part of my story, as well. It was often the little things that were overwhelming. I remember the toothpaste aisle being a sense of "too much", because there were multiple brands, types, and choices. It all seemed unnecessary at the time. The thought of people keeping their doors unlocked was ridiculous, and to this day, I double check all outside doors at night, as I make safety a priority.

Redemption from living in fear came gradually, but it wasn't a passive deliverance. I had to fight for freedom. One night in particular comes to mind. That night, I warred. I contended for my freedom and to believe the truth of Scripture. I knew I needed to get with God and have Him change me, and I knew that I needed the Word. The Scripture was a war tool for me that night. I couldn't tell you if it was 20 minutes or two hours that I paced back and forth in front of the house, warring with Truth and repeating Scripture over myself.

"For God has not given us a spirit of fearfulness, but one of power, love and sound judgment." (2 Timothy 1:7)

I looked up into the sky, could see the darkened night and the stars through the branches of the trees, and back and forth I paced, knowing God would bring me freedom. I warred and I declared the Truths over myself. I didn't stop until I had peace, but when it finally came, I knew the warring was over. I knew there existed a peace that passes understanding and I knew that peace was a part of the Kingdom of God.

> **Don't worry about anything, but in everything, through prayer and petition with thanksgiving, let your requests be made known to God. And the peace of God, which surpasses every thought, will guard your hearts and minds in Christ Jesus. (Philippians 4:6-7)**

That knowledge was enough for me. The exchange of fear for Heaven's peace was a slice of relief I needed in that moment.

Chapter 12: The Ranch

It was a blessing that I returned to Iowa to complete my final year of university after my one year abroad. In retrospect, I look back and see my soul, spirit, and body needed that time and space to heal. It was toward the end of the school year that I went to Wildwood Hills Ranch for my senior year internship, and I wouldn't trade it for anything. It was a Godsend.

I got to work with kids labeled 'at-risk' who shared their stories and their hearts with the staff and with one another. This Wildwood Hills Ranch wasn't just a retreat center or camp; it became a place of healing for many who came as strangers and left as friends.
We creek-stomped, hiked, completed team building activities with our cabin-mates, rode horses, made art collaborations, acted out skits, facilitated a talent show, slid down the slip n slide, canoed, kayaked, fished, and played the famous 'capture the flag'.

We were incredibly active, thus it was a surprise to me when I found myself out of breath, huffing and puffing for air, and barely able to breath as we walked up a slight incline on our way to lunch. This was toward the end of the summer, and we'd been running around playing games and walking everywhere on campus. I had no reason for being out of shape, yet I was struggling to breathe and talk.

I figured it was a fluke and considered taking up running or some extra cardio, but upon returning home from the summer long internship, my mom and I discovered it wasn't actually about me being out of shape. Under no control of my own, I was losing my breath along with my voice.

I was going mute.

It baffled me. I had returned home to complete my senior year at University, had made it through the entire year, and then all of a sudden my body reacted in an unexplainable way. I suddenly struggled to speak, to breathe, and to sing. I would open up my mouth, and air would come out; but sound would not always accompany it. Words were difficult to form, not because I couldn't think of what to say, but because the sound wouldn't come out of my mouth. Stuttering became an issue, and I began to prefer signing and communicating nonverbally, as this was easier. I could sometimes whisper or if the room was deadly silent, I could mouth and articulate a thought. If there were any measurable decibels in the room, I struggled to speak clearly in a manner people could hear me. Talking with grandparents or people who were hard of hearing was painful for everyone in the room.

I don't remember all the details of how long it lasted or where we went for doctor appointments, but I do remember how the Lord helped deliver me from being mute. It was a process and the deliverance and healing came in waves; but I also know the Lord accelerated my healing and started showing me Himself in ways I'd never encountered Him before. He started giving me visions, dreams, and encounters with Him, and when I would pray and process, He would come into past memories and change my perception of feeling unsafe or scared by showing me where He was in that moment. The memory itself wouldn't change, because it was a reality that really did occur at one point; but the awful feelings associated with the memories would begin to dissipate as The Light showed up.

One example of healing the Lord gave me was with JJ. When I was back in the US, I had a season where I was able to process and heal in a healthy, life-giving environment of prayer and worship. This season was one of the best gifts the Lord gave me, because He came and met me where I was. I remember sitting on a couch, feeling the healing presence of the Lord, and being open to whatever it was the Lord wanted to do in me. With my eyes closed, I began to see a storyline in my mind's eye. JJ was walking on the sidewalk in front of my South African apartment heading toward the direction of the sun. My red, drawstring sports bag was on his back, filled with my computer, camera, and the belongings he'd stolen from our house. Jesus was in front of him, redirecting JJ, saying, "no", and telling him to return the stolen items. JJ kept walking and didn't listen, and it's as though he didn't even see the Lord. I saw this picture play out in my head, and I started repenting, telling the Lord I'm sorry that JJ stole my stuff and that he doesn't know any better, is just a kid, and likely needed that stuff to sell to pay off someone who was exploiting him.

Immediately, the Lord said, "No, JJ stole your stuff and I gave that stuff to you. Those things were yours, and you're not trusting Me to provide for JJ and neither is he."

I knew the Lord was correcting my wrong thinking and was helping me to repent (change my mind; think differently) about His provision for not only me, but also for His other children on earth. The Lord is never harsh with me, but occasionally He is firm. This was one of those times.

Chapter 14: Cambodia

The Lord was firm but not harsh. He redirected my thinking, especially in regards to my design, calling, and anointing. I gained the gift of being extremely raw and real with both the Lord and myself. In one conversation, I told the Lord, in all sincerity, that I was not going back on the mission field ever again. I knew He'd spoken to me about nations, about going overseas, and about sharing His glory with others across the world; but the pain I'd encountered in South Africa had left a scar of disappointment on the hopes and dreams in my heart. I made a vow to not pursue missions again. I agreed with the enemy to not fulfill my God given destiny.

That's when God told me to go to Cambodia.

'Cambodia? I don't even know what that is, let alone where that is, assuming it's a place! Cambodia? Lord, seriously?' I thought to myself.

Thanks to Google, I discovered Cambodia is a small country in Southeast Asia. Almost laughing, I shook my head. I had never thought about it, nor had I wanted to go there. Of all the places I'd wanted to visit around the world, the existence of Cambodia wasn't even on my radar.

Apparently that was not a factor for the Lord, because in 2012, my team and I took off work for a three-week intensive trip to Cambodia, where we linked up with Christian nonprofit organizations who worked with justice and anti-trafficking movements. Redemption filled the stories of that trip through and through, and much healing came from being obedient to the Lord's instruction to go overseas again.

One story of healing came from receiving a letter from a teammate who went on the trip with us. Because he had limited time off work, he could only come for two out of the three weeks. He was a thoughtful brother, and he wrote notes to everyone before he left. In his note to me, he explained that part of the reason he came on this trip was to aid and support me in my healing journey.

He had paid thousands of dollars for plane tickets, had taken two weeks' vacation off work, and had flown overseas to an unknown country to aid in my healing. That's love. There was no romantic interest, and he was just a friend. He did it out of love, because it was the heart of Jesus that propelled him.

Being on a team like this is part of what was healing for me. The Lord kept sending people who were trustworthy, full of grace, and were willing to be in process with me. There wasn't a rush to "be healed" or an expectation to get over the therapists' diagnosis of

PTSD, anxiety, and depression. There were no limits in how to interact with God; I just had humans allowing me to be human. That reality coupled with the Lord encountering me by showing up in my memories and in my dreams, hugely impacted my healing journey.

Chapter 15: Basketball Courts

I always had a desire to return to South Africa and was constantly looking for a way to make it happen. In 2015, I was in Israel, for a three-month internship when I found a Youth With A Mission (YWAM) base in Port Elizabeth, South Africa, the same exact city where I had studied abroad in 2009-2010. I contacted the base to discover they'd never hosted a Discipleship Training School (DTS), and that this would be their first time hosting students. This was just like my study abroad experience hosting the first year of the study abroad program. This was the first of many similarities.

I returned to South Africa in February of 2016 to do YWAM, and ended up staying only blocks away from the building where I lived the first semester when I studied abroad. The same convenience store where I used to live across the street in the international student's apartments was a block away and within viewing distance, once I stepped out of the gate of my house. The boardwalk, where I'd met Vuyo at the church service, was within walking distance, and the ocean front view remained the same, only better, after having been renovated by the city. The basketball court where I originally met the boys and fostered a relationship through sports was the same court my YWAM team and I walked to in the afternoons to get out energy after long, morning lectures.

I was at that basketball court in 2016 during my YWAM training school, when I undoubtedly saw someone who looked like JJ, only in an older and more built body. I did a double take, shook it off, and figured it wouldn't be possible, as the odds seemed ridiculous. My attention drew near to the beautiful area, where I sat. There was a large, grassy park, and a place to sit where one could gaze at a man-made pond with a wooden bridge crossing over to the other side. It was a perfect place for an outdoor hiatus, only minutes away from where I lived.

Chapter 16: 4/23

For months, the Lord had been showing me the same numbers over and over again; 4/23. I would see it on the clock, on calendars, on signs as we drove on the road, and on license plates. I don't know what it is about license plates, but the Lord tends to repeat things on license plates and point them out to me. He's very unreligious and outside the box, and I've learned to just go with it when He makes it unmistakably clear.

When I kept seeing 4/23, I didn't know what it meant. I wondered if it was a date or a Scripture reference, and it came up so often that I knew I wasn't making it up. It was everywhere!

When I got to South Africa in February of 2016, the family leading the YWAM base was pregnant with another child. The leaders wanted to celebrate with the YWAM community, and the mother invited all the ladies at the base to a baby shower on the 23rd of April. Typically I'd be very excited to attend, especially as it's a family event, and I love to celebrate with family; but I wasn't feeling well that day and I decided to stay home.

I stayed in the women's bedroom, where it's rare to be in complete silence and solitude with no other women in the room. It's practically unheard of, but this day I had the room all to myself! I was relieved and thanked God for this alone time that I could focus on just Him and I. I could play my own music, journal, and play my ukulele without interruption.

When I realized what day it was, I was even more ecstatic; because I felt like the Lord had set up a date just for Him and I to be together! He'd been talking to me about this day for months, and I wondered what He wanted to show me that was so great He told me months in advance.

I had a sweet time with Him, but hours passed and I was running out of things to say, journal, and play. I only knew so many chords on my ukulele, and I started feeling better, thanked God for the accelerated healing, and ventured out of the house with one of my teammates. This teammate was realistic, easygoing, easy to talk with, and kept things light hearted. It was a blessing and a gift to spend time with him, as there was no language barrier due to both of us being from westernized countries and speaking English. Because of his nationality, he valued fitness highly; therefore he ran a lot and was in good shape. From a distance, you could see that he was a bigger man, and if you didn't know him, you might guess he's the guy on the Mr. Clean commercials. He was bald, had bulging muscles under his white V-neck, and was pasty white. Because I was with him and because he was protective of his teammates, I felt safe.

As the Mr. Clean look-a-like and I strolled down the waterfront, I again saw the boy who looked like an older version of JJ. I kept seeing him everywhere! I saw him near the basketball courts, by the man made pond, crossing the grassy park, and now I was seeing him on the ocean front street we walked on. As I got closer and closer, reality sank in. This grown up version of JJ really could be JJ!

This was crazy to me, as it'd been at least five years since I last saw him. He was on the street helping park cars and was receiving money for watching over them to make sure they didn't get damaged or stolen. He was doing a job older street kids notoriously have, and I saw physical signs he was still using. I knew he was using out of his hunger and need for more than just food; but I'd also grown up in those five years enough to know that the Lord is the One who provides and that not every broken vessel is mine to fix. I had a healthier perspective this time.

I had compassion, but I didn't have sympathy. I embraced empathy, but I did not embrace pity.

I walked up to JJ, asked if he was who I thought he was, and he confirmed. We connected and hugged, and I welcomed him into my presence graciously; but this time I realized I needed healthy boundaries in the relationship. I said nothing about him stealing my stuff, but I did mention I'd prayed for him and I shared with him that the Lord had put him and the other boys on my heart and had given me a couple dreams about them since I'd seen them last.

We spoke for a few minutes, and briefly into the conversation, he asked where I lived and if he could come over. I'd learned my lesson and didn't give away an address or area where we lived; but by the grace of God, I also still had my Mr. Clean look-a-like teammate by my side. I felt no imminent danger around JJ, and I didn't think he would hurt me; but I knew my teammate could and would protect me if anything happened. I also knew the Lord had set me up on this divine appointment on 4/23, because He'd been talking to me about it for months!

That was the last real conversation I had with JJ, and I had resolution, healing, and peace from seeing him again. Even five years later, the Lord knew to set me up. He hadn't forgotten. He let me heal at home in the US, and then he let me conclude and resolve it on South African soil.

All that time, I didn't know 4/23 was a specific date where the Lord's goodness and loving-kindness would manifest. Interestingly enough, if I switch around the numbers to resemble South Africa's format of writing dates to dd/mm/yy, it'd end up being 23/4, which reminds me of Psalm 23:4.

Even when I go through the darkest valley,
I fear no danger,
For You are with me;
Your rod and Your staff—they comfort me.
(Psalm 23:4)

Chapter 17: Miracles, Signs, and Wonders

Our YWAM Discipleship Training School consisted of three months of lecture phase in South Africa followed by three months of outreach. Our specific team was sent to Malawi, Africa, which is a few countries north of South Africa. There we gained experience in different types of ministries. We went to nearby villages with interpreters and prayed for people, and though I almost always lacked understanding of the words that were spoken, I could see the impact on people's hearts. I witnessed visible signs in people's bodies that showed the Lord was working in them. Some people would cry, others would visibly shake, and some would react and fall on the ground as the Lord did deep healing in their souls and spirits.

Another ministry at the base was born out of a compassionate heart of one of the leaders at the base. He had a heart for women who'd been widowed, and this propelled him to start a ministry for the widowed women in the village. One day our school walked with him to the village, where we met the women and shucked corn with them while listening to their personal stories and testimonies. This particular day was not filled with people shaking and falling on the ground. It was about the simplicity of having compassion on neighboring people. Not every ministry was loud, experientially new, or outside of the box. Sometimes we were simply there to love people and do life with them.

When we visited Ntaja, a remote village with a few streetlights and no billboards, our team members connected with the hosts and were drawn into the culture. Perhaps it was something about the simplicity that drew us. The nighttime sky elongated every direction into a star show I'd never before seen. Shooting stars paraded the dark night like peaceful fireworks, declaring the glory of God. The peacefulness in the villages welcomed a kind hospitality that quickly made strangers friends. The hour plus long bike rides into locally claimed "nearby" villages became worth the fight against breaking bicycle gears when we saw faces of Bible study attendees who were hungry to hear the Word of God.

The Ntaja YWAM base was a family of faithful followers of Jesus who lived in a predominantly Muslim village. Many villagers could not read, and especially the women were not educated. Because of this, they didn't know the Quran well or at all and likely had mixed religious beliefs influenced by their culture.

There were a few churches in the village, and some of them asked us to come speak. They gladly accepted us, and we were able to preach about Jesus and the Gospel to some who had never heard about Him.

There was hunger and curiosity, and the Lord had stirred the people's hearts before we arrived. One woman at a Bible study said she'd had two dreams. One dream showed a wide path and a narrow path. Many people were on the wide path, but not many were on the narrow path. She wondered what this dream meant.

Eyes wide and alert, we recognized the Scripture the Lord had directly communicated to her, and we read it together as a group.

> **"Enter through the narrow gate. For wide is the gate and broad is the road that leads to destruction, and many enter through it. But small is the gate and narrow the road that leads to life, and only a few find it. (Matthew 7:13-14 NIV)**

We then discussed the passage and explained that the pathway to Jesus is narrow and leads to life. The message was simple and seemed to be understood. Jesus is an incredibly good communicator.

She shared a second dream where she saw people in white robes, dancing, singing, and full of joy. She didn't know why they had such joy and didn't understand why they were happy or what they were doing. She was curious and wanted to know more about the meaning of this dream.

Again, being amazed at Jesus' communication with her through these dreams, we found Scriptures that explained His teachings. We explained that the book of Revelation describes scenes in Heaven and that there are people dressed in white robes who are worshiping and praising God. We explained they were full of joy because they loved being with Jesus and His family in Heaven, and they were celebrating with God.

> **After this I looked, and there was a vast multitude from every nation, tribe, people, and language, which no one could number, standing before the throne and before the Lamb. They were robed in white with palm branches in their hands. And they cried out in a loud voice:**
> **Salvation belongs to our God,**
> **who is seated on the throne,**
> **and to the Lamb!**
> **All the angels stood around the throne, the elders, and the four living creatures, and they fell facedown before the throne and worshiped God, saying:**
> **Amen! Blessing and glory and wisdom**
> **and thanksgiving and honor**
> **and power and strength**
> **be to our God forever and ever. Amen.**
> **(Revelation 7:9-12)**

The simplicity and ease of sharing the Gospel in this Bible study was amazing, because there was a hunger and the Lord had stirred up people's hearts prior to our coming. It was a blessing to everyone, and we rejoiced in the Lord's pursuit of His Beloved.
Bible studies like these happened on a regular basis, and miracles were a part of Christian's lives.

In one of the Bible studies we visited there was a small child who had bad dreams and was feeling side effects from the nighttime terrors. She was scared, and the ladies in the community asked that we pray for her to have relief from these bad dreams. Believing for her healing, we prayed for her. When we came back a week or two later, her demeanor was completely different and the community reported that the Lord had heard our prayers and she had been healed, with no bad dreams recurring! They testified that the girl had much more joy and life after we prayed for her. Jesus was doing a work in this little girl, and the entire Bible study group acknowledged it. It reminds me of Scriptures where Jesus did miracles in front of people to show them His nature, that they might believe.

These signs, miracles, and wonders also increased my belief in God; because I saw the theology I read about in Scripture being played out in daily life. One of the ministries I hope to never forget includes riding in the back of a bakkie for what seemed like hours to get to a remote village to show a Jesus film. It'd be miraculous if I could ever find the way there again, because we traveled from the remote village of Ntaja to even more unreached places out in the boondocks of African country land. It was beautiful, and I wondered if we were amidst animals we should be watching out for; but I was so incredibly happy to be doing what I knew I was called to do that it didn't matter. Never before had I felt such an alignment with fulfilling my life purpose. I was in the African boondocks, and the Lord was satisfying the dreams He'd placed in me while I was a young girl.

When we arrived in the village, there were brown, dirt roads and a myriad of trees surrounding thatched roof homes. The simplicity of the layout reminded me of a park where there was space to wander and breath and ponder; there was space to take in the beauty of nature and likeness of God. It was serene and there was peace in the air, tangible like a refreshing breeze communicating the still, small voice of God. Stopping to take it all in, I breathed, enjoying the presence in that moment, enjoying the evening to come, and watching the sunset fall beyond the tree lines brushing the sky with pastels and gentle light.

Our team watched the sky's natural light fade beyond the horizon as the night brought the theatre's natural moonlight to our aid. Once the stars showed and the moon became our natural light, it was time to roll the film.

With the generator plugged in, the projector began to roll the video on the white sheet pulled taught between two wooden poles. The local language read below the scenes of Jesus and His disciples, and I heard the crowd engage with emotional "oohs", "aahs", and laughter.

Eyes peered up at the sky, I saw the expanse of God's reach among the stars. Breathing in the fresh air, I filled my lungs with satisfaction of a beautiful night at an outdoor theatre. I felt the children leaning on me as we sat in the front row on the dusty ground in front of the standing adults. The humility of this moment as kids squeezed in to sit by me to feel my white skin and touch my hair was hilarious, familiar, and soul satisfying. This is what I had dreamed of all my life.

I beamed with proud affirmation as a few of my teammates got up to speak after the film's end. They explained the Gospel and talked about Jesus and what the movie depicted. The translator translated for the crowd, and the people nodded and responded verbally as they heard the Gospel in their own tongue.

Afterward, many people came up, wanting prayer, and the majority asked for head and stomach pains to be healed. The faith in that place was incredible! They'd just heard about Jesus, and they believed He could heal, therefore they asked. It was simple, profound, and effective.

I didn't hear the testimony that night, but later on, my team informed me that they prayed for a little boy who was deaf, and the Lord immediately healed Him! It was an amazing miracle, and is one I share and remind myself of when I am praying for healing for others or myself. Jesus still heals. He's in the business of restoring all things, big and small.

Chapter 18: I'll follow You Anywhere, Coach

Some Scriptures become life long Truths that resonate deep within my soul. Psalm 16 is one of these life Scriptures for me, and I can see how the Lord has counseled me at night.

"I will praise the Lord, who counsels me; even at night my heart instructs me."
(Psalm 16:7 NIV)

Sometimes I don't realize the Lord instructs me in the night time, and this is when I've gained help from my roommates who lovingly inform me I woke them up in the middle of the night, jabbering away in my sleep. This happened one night while we were fast asleep under our mosquito nets in the YWAM base in Ntaja. My roommate awoke to my talking, and fortunately, she clearly heard what I said.

"I'll follow You anywhere, coach!" I said, before I mumbled something else and returned to my slumber.

The next morning she asked what I was dreaming about in my sleep. Still half asleep, I responded, "I'm not sure. I don't remember. Why do you ask?"

She proceeded to tell me she woke up while we were asleep, because I was yakking away in the middle of the night and she thought I might be speaking to her. Fortunately, she'd heard what I had said, because I didn't have any recollection of it.

At the moment I didn't have much context or understanding for what it meant, but I wrote it all down in order that I could reference it later. Note to self - keep writing down dreams and encounters with the Lord, as it might be a helpful puzzle piece for the future.

Chapter 19: Return to Me

And afterward, I will pour out my Spirit on all people. Your sons and daughters will prophesy, your old men will dream dreams, your young men will see visions.
(Joel 2:28)

I am thankful I wrote it down, because it ended up making more sense later on when I had a dream that helped to connect the dots. I had the dream during a whirlwind weekend, when my friends and I decided to take a spontaneous road trip from Nebraska to Colorado to visit a friend who was attending a missions conference. Unbeknownst to us, our other friends were also there, and we embraced them with hugs and celebration when we ran into them after not having seen them for a long while. We had a mini reunion with mission-minded, Jesus loving friends, and the weekend was full of reminiscing, dreaming, and praying for nations and for the Lord to move in different places on the earth. It again stirred the fire in my heart to be in the nations and to return to South Africa. I'd been talking about this with the Lord, bringing it before Him again, asking Him to satisfy the desires He placed in me long ago.

My friends and I were discussing this renewed, fiery passion on our 10 plus hour drive back to Nebraska, and I started telling them about South Africa and how the Lord was stirring my heart to go back. I had just recently returned to the states from South Africa, and the experience had been neither easy nor smooth; but it was the Lord's grace that gave me a desire to go back. In telling my friends this, I remembered the dream.

In my dream, a woman was teaching netball in South Africa. I was with her when she wanted to get certified to have a coaching license. I felt like I'd seen her or had met her before in my dream, and I was interested to connect with her. I first saw her on a dirt road, but when she was speaking to me about the certification, she was behind a piece of furniture, either a chair or a couch. I think we were in her house, and we were inside when she told me about the certification. She may have also been working with street children while in South Africa.

As I told my friends this dream from the backseat of the Toyota, I began to explain that the woman in my dream was in South Africa, and in everyday life (not in the dream), was from one of my favorite movies, called Return to Me. That's when I put two and two together. Return to Me. South Africa.

Chapter 20: The Pieces Come Together

As imaginable, I was ecstatic in the car when I put these two pieces together, because I knew the Lord was talking to me about going back to South Africa. You may as well have told me I won the lottery. I was a simultaneous emotional, happy, hot mess in the back seat of that Toyota.

It wasn't until recently that I knew about the vision on the Lord's heart, including the possibility of returning to South Africa. Within the last couple of years, the Lord has connected me with people in South Africa who have the same heart and vision I do. The similarities are so incredibly specific, that I'm convinced the Lord has connected us. My friends in South Africa have a heart for prayer and worship, permaculture, family, restoration, mentoring youth, living a healthy lifestyle, and of all things, they like basketball! That's not a common hobby in South Africa, and I became ecstatic when I discovered their love for the sport! It's one of those unexpected, specific gifts from the Lord that puts the cherry on top. It's the abundance of the goodness of God!

He is way better than I have believed. There's no way I could have connected all of the currently moving puzzle pieces myself. Perhaps learning that God really is as good as He says He is, is part of the joy of growing in faith. His kind of response to my prayers beckons me to dream more. His faithfulness in answering my prayers has increased my faith in who He says He is. It's definitely a season of dreaming big and asking the Lord for things that are bigger than we could ask or imagine. I know He'll always outdo my expectations.

It's easy to believe that when I look back and have perspective of hindsight. When I take a step back and look at the big picture perspective, I see the Lord's faithfulness. Just like anyone else, it's still a fight to believe in His goodness and to know that He's for me and will pull through in current seasons.

Moving forward to the present season I am in now, I can see His goodness. I see His goodness when I am singing and speaking, knowing that He has healed me and brought back my voice in order that I can declare His worthiness and give praise back to Him. I see His goodness when I meet people who talk about having anxiety and depression, and I speak, confidently, about how the Lord has healed me of both. I see His goodness in being able to pray for people and see peace fall over them as they give their anxieties and worries to the Lord.

The Truth is I am no longer mute, and the Lord is continuing to heal me and speak and sing through me. What the enemy tried to take away in the form of my voice, Jesus has released through me abundantly. Songs and poems, books and loads of creativity are flowing from me, because Jesus is faithful to complete what He started. He will have His way. He will not let His children be trampled. Jesus will have the final word. It will be good and true. He will reign victoriously.

My testimony of being healed by Jesus is one of many stories of His goodness, and there are many yet to be experienced, written, and shared.

Recently my friend and I moved out of state to be closer to a community of people who intentionally get before the Lord to worship and pray and seek His face. They live out Psalm 27:4 in a beautiful way.

> **I have asked one thing from the Lord;**
> **it is what I desire:**
> **to dwell in the house of the Lord**
> **all the days of my life,**
> **gazing on the beauty of the Lord**
> **and seeking Him in His temple.**
> **(Psalm 27:4)**

I am in this place, even now, as I write. Here, I get to intentionally be before the Lord and have both literal and figurative blank pages, where I ask again and again for His confirmation. I want His full and complete instruction. I want every piece of advice and wisdom from God that He wants to speak to me in this season. I do not want anything of my own agenda unless He placed it there in the first place. I want the Lord's direction and instruction, hence why I am taking an intentional season to spend time with the

Lord and to make sure my heart is right before Him, here in the place of prayer and worship.

My friend, whom I mentioned in the introduction of this book, and myself have been seeking the Lord. He's been giving clarity through His Word, through prayer, through dreams, and He's confirmed to us through other Saints. He's spoken again and again about different locations on earth that are on His heart. I am excited to keep the conversation going and to sit before Him, again, asking Him what He wants us to do, where to go, when, and with whom. May I be a ready scribe, ever carefully taking note of what He says.

My heart is moved by a noble theme
As I recite my verses to the king;
my tongue is the pen of a skillful writer.
(Psalm 45:1)

The Lord answered me:
Write down this vision; clearly inscribe it on tablets
so one may easily read it.
(Habakkuk 2:2)

I believe everyone's story is one the Lord wants to have a hand in writing, and anyone can give testimonies about how the Lord has worked in their lives. If this is the encouragement you need to write your own story, let it stand as a billboard sign before you, flashing in neon colored lights to share your testimonies and stories, as well.

For you, readers, and for my basketball girls, my prayer is that you all would be MVP's of Heaven, and that God would look down on you and smile, knowing that He gets to do life together with you. May you be more familiar and intimate with God and the Kingdom of Heaven all of your days, more than any other thing. Amen.

To My Basketball Girls

To my basketball girls who've attended camps, practices, open gyms, and games:

You are a value of Heaven. You are treasured, wanted, loved, and found immeasurably important in Heaven. You are of great significance. You are bought. You have been paid for. Heaven was found without the Messiah for 33 years, because the Father considered you important to fight for and buy back with the blood of His own Son. You are a value of Heaven.

You are treasured, because you are a gem, unlike any other person on earth. You are the only who can worship and pour your heart out to God with your honest, raw adoration. No other person can worship God today, right now, the way you can with the testimonies and personal experiences you've had with the Lord. Your worship is valuable and worthy of giving to God. Only you can give Him your worship. No one else can do that for you, and no one else can worship Him the way you were made to worship Him. Every aspect of your worship is unique, and it touches the Father's heart to receive your adoration.

You are loved. You are made in the image of a Jealous Lover.

You are found immeasurably important. Your price was paid by immeasurable value.

You are of great significance. A Judge deemed you as God's inheritance.

You are bought. You're worth chasing after and fighting for.

You have been paid for; it was God's desire to have you with Him forever.

My prayer is that you become and remain His forever and ever, and that one day, I'll be able to worship Jesus with you again in person! Until then, I hope and pray you know you're loved and wanted, because you, precious daughter, are a value of heaven.

May you know and walk in Truth, and may you be completely well in your spirit, soul, and body. Amen.

You are a joy, and I have loved being your coach. I am proud of you! Stay pyped!

Made in the USA
Columbia, SC
15 August 2022

65237260R10050